TWELVE BRAIN PRINCIPLES
THAT MAKE THE DIFFERENCE

In A Nutshell

s e r i e s

TWELVE BRAIN PRINCIPLES
THAT MAKE THE DIFFERENCE

In A Nutshell
collection

Brian M. Pete • Robin J. Fogarty

Skyhorse Publishing

Skyhorse Publishing books may be purchased in bulk at special discounts for sales promotion, corporate gifts, fund-raising, or educational purposes. Special editions can also be created to specifications. For details, contact the Special Sales Department, Skyhorse Publishing, 307 West 36th Street, 11th Floor, New York, NY 10018 or info@skyhorsepublishing.com.

Skyhorse® and Skyhorse Publishing® are registered trademarks of Skyhorse Publishing, Inc.®, a Delaware corporation.

Visit our website at www.skyhorsepublishing.com.

10 9 8 7 6 5 4 3 2 1

Library of Congress Cataloging-in-Publication Data is available on file.

Print ISBN: 978-1-63450-359-4
Ebook ISBN: 978-1-5107-0131-1

Printed in China

Contents

Acknowledgments

On a theoretical note, of all the information available about how the brain works, perhaps one of the most insightful pieces for educators is the meta-analysis of the research on the brain and learning by Renate and Geoffrey Caine. The twelve principles that govern how the brain learns and remembers provide an invaluable guide for instructional decision making. For their magnificent contribution and generous spirit, we are grateful to the Caines.

On a more practical note, we are grateful to the many hearts, hands, and minds who have made this book possible, especially Dara Lee Howard, who has provided organization, editing and, at times, some writing, and Jon Hensley, who has created a striking cover. To all, our heartfelt thanks.

Brian M. Pete
Robin J. Fogarty

Dedication

With love,

to Maple Ann,

strong and presiding,

like the maple tree

on Maple Hill Road

■□■□■

Introduction

There is the cartoon about the little boy who brags to his friend about how he has taught his dog, Stripe, how to whistle. Subsequently, he replies to the "Doubting Thomas" friend, who points out that Stripe is not whistling, "I said I taught him. I didn't say he learned it." To the authors, this picture is worth a thousand words, as the saying goes. It epitomizes the entirety of the teaching/learning process. Teachers teach! But students must learn! These are two very different sides of the same coin.

This book is part of a two-book series. The first book in the set is titled *Nine Best Practices That Make the Difference* and focuses on the teaching part of the teaching/learning process. This book, *Twelve Brain Principles That Make the Difference*, focuses on the learning part of the teaching/learning equation.

More specifically, this book is about how the brain learns best and all the things teachers can do to facilitate the learning part of the teaching scene. This "Nutshell" presents a unique organization of Renate and Geoffrey Caine's twelve brain principles. The twelve principles are arranged in four specific quadrants as shown in Figure Intro.1. Each quadrant speaks to a particular aspect of the high-achieving classroom and highlights how instructional decisions are governed by the twelve principles.

Climate *for* Learning Challenge/Threat Emotions/Cognition Focused/Peripheral	Skills *of* Learning Parts/Whole Spatial/Rote Parallel Processing
Interactions *With* Learning Physiology Brain Uniqueness Social/Experience	Learning *About* Learning Meaning Patterning Conscious/Unconscious

Figure Intro.1. Four quadrants of brain principles.

Quadrant 1 addresses the environment for learning, stressing both the emotional climate and the enriched environment. This quadrant includes three complementary principles that foster a climate for optimal learning: Principle 1 addresses the concept of challenge engaging the mind; Principle 2 discusses the link between emotions and cognition; and Principle 3 highlights the learning environment and its role in the focused attention and peripheral perception of students.

Quadrant 2 speaks to the standards of learning and the context, content, and process skills for which each K-12 teacher is accountable. Embedded in the concept of necessary concepts and skills for various grade levels or disciplines are the three accompanying principles: Principle 4, which notes that the brain learns parts and whole simultaneously; Principle 5, which documents the rote and spatial memory systems; and Principle 6, which discusses the role of the brain as a parallel processor. All three of these principles speak to the teaching techniques that foster memory and learning.

Quadrant 3 encompasses the concept of hands-on learning that is constantly and continually facilitated as an integral part of any lesson. Included in this quadrant are three principles that dictate ways needed to address the eager learner: Principle 7, which highlights the need for being aware of the entire physiology in the learning setting; Principle 8, which acknowledges the difference in the structure and chemistry of each and every brain and pushes the implications of that diversity for classroom teachers; and Principle 9, which explores the concept of the social brain and how it learns easily when embedded in experiences. All three of these principles inform the practice of hands-on learning.

Quadrant 4 focuses on reflective thinking and how the brain makes meaning, stores information, and retrieves needed memories. Again, three principles make up the essence of this quadrant. Principle 10 clarifies the nature of the brain to seek meaning; Principle 11 discusses the role of patterning in memory and learning; and Principle 12 reminds the teacher of the need for processing time—down time—for the brain to complete its deep processing of new input. All three principles illuminate the idea of how the brain makes sense of the world. All three speak to the practices of the skillful teacher.

How the Book Is Organized

The book is organized in four parts that parallel the four quadrants: Climate for Learning, Skills of Learning, Interactions With Learning, and Learning About Learning. Within each part, each principle in the quadrant is fully explained. To start, each principle is introduced by "unpacking" the language through the use of synonyms. In addition, each of the principles is discussed through the use of three distinct parts: A Story to Tell, Things You Need to Know, and A Tiny Transfer to Try.

In the first section, "A Story to Tell," synonyms, analogies, and a visual icon are backdrops to the story that opens the discussion. The story illustrates the essence of each principle in folksy, everyday language. The purpose of the story is to capture the motivation recognized in this short poem:

Tell me a fact and I'll learn.
Tell me the truth and I'll believe.
But, tell me a story and it will
live in my heart forever.

In the next section, "Things You Need to Know," two questions give the reader basic information about the principle. First, What's It All About? presents factual information, and second, Why Bother? discusses the rationale and implications for using it in the classroom.

Finally, "A Tiny Transfer to Try" gives teachers a practical application to use immediately in their classrooms or a practice exercise to do in a workshop.

■ □ ■ □ ■

PART ONE: CLIMATE FOR LEARNING

Although the Caines make it quite clear that their twelve principles are a systemic set of principles, the authors have chosen to subdivide the twelve into four distinct but interrelated groups: Climate for Learning, Skills of Learning, Interactions With Learning, and Learning About Learning.

The first group of principles under the heading "Climate for Learning" includes three principles that stress both a safe emotional climate and a sensory rich environment. Principle 1, Challenge engages the mind; threat inhibits the cognitive abilities, talks about the role of rigor in the learning environment. Principle 2, Emotions and cognition are linked, addresses the idea that learning is enhanced in an emotionally safe climate. Finally, Principle 3, The brain learns both through focused attention and peripheral perception, speaks to the idea of a learning environment that is both sensory-rich and print-rich, attracting the focused and peripheral attention of the learner.

In sum, all three principles seem to relate to the emotional culture of the learning environment. Is it emotionally safe to take a risk? Are there many stimuli to spark the growth of dendrites?

■ □ ■ □ ■

Challenge/Threat: Learning Principle 1

Learning Principle 1:	Learning is enhanced by challenge and inhibited by threat.

A Story to Tell

It is the first day of school and the fourth grade teacher is talking to his class about the upcoming school year. The school, which is in a tough urban neighborhood, has been on probation for three years. The teacher says, "The reading and writing skills and habits that we will work on this year will be important for you when you get to college."

All of the students look up; many raise their hands. The first student who is called on asks, "How long is college?"

Another asks, "Who can go to college?"

The teacher moves to the side of the room and begins writing on another chalkboard, in a more prominent place. As he moves, students turn in their chairs and follow him with their eyes.

Synonyms — Challenge

Responsibility

Obligation

Duty

Venture

Formidable task

Problem

Synonyms — Threat

Hazard

Intimidation

Fear

Pressure

Anxiety

Concern

As he is writing, he says, "Four years from now you will enter high school (he writes 4 on the board), and then after two years of high school (he writes a 2 on the board), you will begin to consider colleges and universities that you might like to attend. After you graduate from high school (he writes another 2 on the board), you will enter a four-year college (he writes a 4 on the board). The teacher continues the timeline all the way through medical school and then asks, "How many years will it take you to become a doctor?"

A few hands go up, the teacher calls on them, but no one has the answer. Then, in the back row, one boy, who has not spoken at all this first day because of his poor English skills, raises his hand and says, "Twenty years."

"That's right!" says the teacher, and all the other students turn and look at the boy in the back row.

Later the same day the teacher is handing papers to the students and as he passes the boy who answered correctly, the teacher leans in and says, "Here you go, Doctor."

Things You Need to Know

What's It All About?

Challenge is a test of one's abilities or resources in a demanding but stimulating undertaking, for example, undertaking a demanding career. *Threat* is an indication of impending danger or harm, for example, seeing lightning while playing golf.

Challenge

A classroom environment designed for learning has to challenge and at the same time not threaten learners. This may sound like a simple goal, but on the first day of school, as the room fills with children who are together for the first time, the environment can appear threatening. It does not have to. By presenting the new beginning as a challenge, teachers can fire students' brains and watch them come alive. This human need for challenge is a primal force that teachers can tap. Research on the brain shows that humans like challenge.

This human need for challenge is a primal force that teachers can tap.

When students are challenged with rigorous curriculum, they respond with enthusiasm. Challenge, when presented in a way that allows each student to imagine being "in the game" and able to "bring something to the table," creates the kind of classroom that fosters student engagement and achievement.

Challenging problems that also have emotional relevance are a natural hook for learning. When students are faced with a problem that has no easy answer, teachers can help them to persevere, become engaged, and work hard to solve the problem.

There are endless stories about someone who has been told that he or she can't do something—for example, "This problem is for students in the next grade; it's a level above you"— but succeeds because he or she sees it as a challenge, not an impediment. A well-thought-out challenge from a teacher can engage students, who then work harder than they ever could have imagined they could to achieve their goal.

■ □ ■ □ ■

Threat

The second part of this principle—Learning . . . inhibited by threat—focuses on the importance of the emotional state of learners as they try to learn. Faced with threat— threat of danger, threat of embarrassment, threat of shame—a human's brain is dominated by the emotional brain and may not function to its potential in the cognitive realm.

Goleman's (1995) discussion of emotional intelligence emphasizes that when students feel supported and safe in the classroom, they are more likely to perform to a higher level. On the other hand, students who feel that there is a threat of any kind become emotionally charged, and thus, their cognitive abilities take second place.

A threatening situation may be one in which a student has to give an oral report in front of the class. The student may sabotage her own success just so she can avoid this emotionally threatening possibility. On the other hand, a student member of a cooperative group may rise to the challenge of his role as spokesperson for the group because he knows, as part of the group, that he is not alone and, thus, feels more comfortable and less threatened.

The difference between a rigorous challenge and a threatening situation is both simple and complex.

The difference between a rigorous challenge and a threatening situation is both simple and complex. A challenge might be so tough that learners fail in their efforts and collapse in nervous frustration. This is a rigorous challenge gone awry and turned into a threatening situation. But, when the challenge is structured correctly, learners can find a solution after a

■ □ ■ □ ■

reasonable amount of work by using tools they have mastered even though the task is pushing their envelope of skills. These students are challenged but not threatened; they feel safe and even free to risk failure or, at least, temporary failure. This experimenting and stretching of their capacity to understand and make meaning is the best possible way for them to learn.

Students quickly diagnose a poorly designed learning situation as a possible threat, particularly if they see failure as fatal or maiming. If their wrong answers are to be posted on the board for all the class to see, students may not be able to produce the right answer, even though they may actually know it. If the outcome of a test means that they are separated in some way from their peers, students may lose their capacity to process information at peak levels, and they may even sabotage their own chances for success just to feel like they are in control of their own destiny.

Why Bother?

A classroom that challenges students to think with rigor, is the classroom of high expectations (Haycock, 1999). In fact, when low performing schools are staffed with quality teachers who expect rigorous thinking and complex solutions, even the lowest performing students will rise to the occasion (Haycock, 1999). The learner simply cannot resist the look of a good challenge and his or her mind goes into high gear (Sprenger, 1999).

When complex problems are part of the enriched environment, students will encounter, without fanfare and quite naturally, problems that they cannot solve. For example, when intricate puzzles, word games, and brainteasers are a regular part of the classroom, students can interact with them on their own time and in their own way. When they encounter a visual spatial problem, a mathematics quiz, or a hands-on manipulative that they cannot immediately conquer, they have a chance to demonstrate curiosity, even failure, without high stakes. Figure 1.1 suggests kinds of problems and decisions that may be created to challenge rigorously, but also safely and frequently.

Problem Solving	Decision Making	Creative Ideation
Mathematics problem solving	Ethical dilemmas	Science projects
Future problem solving	Moral issues	Presentations
Olympics of the mind	Values clarification	Persuasive speech
Service learning	Character building	Artistic murals
Problem based learning	Court decisions	Musical compositions
Civic projects	Debating	Map making
Choose your own ending	Athletic competition	Conceptualizing a museum

Figure 1.1. Safe challenges.

A Tiny Transfer to Try

Challenge or Threat: A Fine Line

Attach poster paper to the walls in the corners of the room (if possible). Each poster shows a different challenging puzzle, for example:

■ □ ■ □ ■

1. A Mathematics Story Problem

Rachel has six more brothers than she has sisters, but her brother Ryan has four more brothers than he has sisters. If there are fewer than 10 children in the family, how many boys and girls are there?

2. A Tongue Twisting Poem

Jim had a small baseball card collection. All but five were signed, all but five were rookie cards, and all but five were less than 10 years old. What is the minimum number of cards he could have had?

3. A Geometric Line Drawing

Unscramble the letters in each segment in the "pie." Find the missing letter that completes each word and is shown by a "?" (use the same letter for each word)

4. A Riddle

Find the word that fits the first definition, and then add an "S" in front of it to make a new word that matches the second definition. Definitions: Place an "S" in front of a metal container and get a word meaning to glance at. Place and "S" in front of a pixie and get a form of reference.

Ask participants to move around the room in pairs and pick a problem to solve. They are to be prepared to present their answers to the whole group.

After 10 or 15 minutes, ask those that have chosen each problem to meet in different corners of the room and confer and, in a non-threatening way, come to an agreement on the answer.

After each group gives its answers, discuss the level of threat each group or individual experienced and how they think it affected performance. Use the Aha!—Oh, no! chart shown in Figure 1.2 to record some of the responses.

Aha! What worked?	Oh, no! What was threatening?

Figure 1.2. Aha!—Oh, no! chart.

Emotions/Cognition: Learning Principle 2

Learning Principle 2:	Emotions are critical to cognitive patterning.

A Story to Tell

The five seventh-grade boys stood at the edge of the fast-moving mountain stream, with their arms folded, stomping their feet to stay warm. This part of their real-world science project was not turning out like they had hoped. The plan was to ride and observe the mountain stream. It was still cold at 8 a.m. They were in the shade of tall fir trees, and they had pulled down the sleeves of their sweatshirts to cover their hands. In the inflatable raft, their instructor was busy preparing to guide them down the river.

The instructor stopped what he was doing and looked up at his students, "Hey, you about ready to go?"

"It's too cold," they muttered.

The teacher stepped up to the boys and said, "Let's go over our procedures."

Synonyms — Cognitive

Mind

Thought

Awareness

Ideas

Abstractions

Logic

Synonyms — Emotions

Feelings

Impressions

Experiences

Intuitions

Sympathy

The students were slow to respond. The teacher threw five life preservers at the boys' feet.

"Guys," he called out, "We need to go over the procedures for running this river; otherwise, it will not be a safe trip and I will have done a poor job as your river guide."

One of the boys said, "Let's go, Mr. Jacobs. I thought we would be floating in the sun with our shirts off. I'm freezing here."

Mr. Jacobs replied, as he reached into the raft for the bailing bucket, "OK, now, the first thing you have to remember about running the river is that you may get wet, so keep your notebooks dry. Are they secured in your pack?"

The boys stuffed their notebooks deep into their packs as Mr. Jacobs filled the bailing bucket with icy mountain water. Before the boys could look up, Mr. Jacobs threw the bucket of cold water, splashing all five of the boys in the face. They jumped and screeched and ran back up the bank of the river trying to catch their breath.

Smiling to himself and remembering the principle that emotions drive attention, Mr. Jacobs says, "OK, now that I have your attention, let's go over the rules for running this river."

Things You Need to Know

What's It All About?

There are two areas inextricably linked: cognitive patterns and emotions. Cognitive patterns are models or originals used as archetypes. Patterns can be a design of natural or maybe of accidental origin. They are a plan, diagram, or model to be followed in making sense of a problem or new situation.

> **Emotion drives attention, attention drives cognition, and cognition drives memory.**

On the other hand, emotions are mental states that arise spontaneously rather than through conscious effort and often are accompanied by physiological changes or a psychological feeling. In the classroom, these two areas are inseparable. Emotion drives attention, attention drives cognition, and cognition drives memory. And, memory is the only evidence of learning.

Students' emotional response to learning determines how well they will retain the information they are trying to learn. Emotions are the gatekeepers to the intellect and, as such, are the primary determinants of what information makes its way to short-term and, eventually, long-term memory.

As an example, think of the emotional center of the brain as the sense of smell and taste when we consider eating a new or unusual food. If it doesn't smell familiar to something we already like, then we may not try it. If we do taste the food, we only continue if we like the flavors. Emotions serve a similar role in the brain and learning process. The brain judges the relevance of information based on emotional history, gives this information the focus that it feels it deserves, and then values the information as it tries fitting it into established patterns created through prior learning.

The emotions related to effective cognition involve more than just pleasure. Relevance can be determined when the learner values the information because of experience and sees the learning as important. New information that does not connect is less likely to be valued or to be added to the patterns that the brain has created.

Learners work with confidence in solving vexing problems, if those problems fit a pattern they are familiar with. When the problem appears hard, learners may be emotionally excited by the prospect of solving it, especially when they have experience with the patterns they are encountering. The brain makes meaning when it can recognize patterns that have been established through past learning, and when they can connect new information to existing patterns.

What the brain knows helps it learn. How the brain has organized and categorized what it knows in the past is how the brain will attempt to organize and categorize what it is trying to know in the present. The brain is constantly making sense of new information by making associations, finding relevance, or seeing connections to past experience, and it does this all in an emotional context.

Why Bother?

When students are encouraged to make meaning in their own way they are more likely to be emotionally prepared to accept new understanding. For example, the cliché writing assignment given early in the beginning of the school year—"What I did on my summer vacation"—is an example of tapping into the emotion and memory of the students. What they remember has an emotional value, and that value is reflected in how well they remember a particular aspect of their summer vacation. What they recall probably has powerful emotional hooks.

Tap into the emotion and memory of the students.

The connections that can be made between prior and new learning are more than just memory. Parnes (1975) says that if teachers ask two questions, they take learning to a new level. These questions are "How does this relate to what you already know?" and "How might you use this in the future?" This simple two-question strategy helps students tap into prior knowledge. If the knowledge is in long-term memory, then it retains the emotional value present at the time the information was new. If the knowledge was valuable enough to remember, then the second question, "How might you use this in the future?" tends to transfer the emotional value to the new learning situation.

Teachers know that, for learning, it is imperative that children feel safe in the classroom. They should feel safe enough to try new things, safe enough to allow their thinking to be visible, and safe enough to challenge and go beyond where they think they can.

For learning, it is imperative that children feel safe.

Lessons learned at the knee of a favorite relative are prime examples of an emotionally safe environment being conducive to learning. A child who trusts someone accepts new information with a higher value as the brain slots that information into long-term memory. The learner wants to remember these lessons because they felt good as they learned these lessons.

A classroom that honors many learning styles is more likely to tap into all the possible ways that students learn and store memories and information. Students who work with their hands to understand more deeply the connections between specific facts and concepts may not be able to prove what they know if asked to recite from memory in front of the class. They may have more success showing what they know with a hands-on demonstration. If students are readers, then they like to read and learn through reading. When given the chance to read, they do. When verbal learners are given the chance to discuss, debate, or give a speech, they will jump at the chance to talk. Students who are strong in mathematics know they feel good when faced with a problem involving numbers, theorems, or equations.

The emotional brain moves from the entry points of learning to process and value information in a complex way. This process is helped when teachers clearly identify the relevance of the learning to the class content or, perhaps, to the test. When the student believes that what they are learning is important to something in their future, then there is an intrinsic motivation to learn. Students who are focused and engaged in the problem are students who have an emotional connection to what they are learning.

Information stored through an emotionally pleasant experience will be emotionally pleasant to recall, to connect to, or to add to. Furthermore, information stored in the context of an emotionally unpleasant experience, although unpleasant to recall, holds the same emotional weight in terms of ability to recall. The emotions, positive or negative, form the context of the cognitive pattern. Figure 2.1 shows some of the experiences that produce emotional hooks to learning for learners.

Positive Connections	Negative Connections
High interest topics	Accountability
Relevance to students	Timelines
Student choices	Deadlines
Cooperative work	Due dates
	Tests and quizzes

Figure 2.1. Emotional hooks to learning.

A Tiny Transfer to Try

The Right Way

In a workshop or classroom setting, using pairs, ask participants to take turns recalling a time when they were so mad that they could not see straight or a time when they were really emotionally caught in the anger syndrome of narrow focus, less reasoning, more emotion, and physical intensity. Ask them to recall the actions they took in that situation.

Then, ask them to discuss with their partners how appropriate their responses were. Where they mad (1) with the right person? (2) in the right way? (3) with the right information? or (4) with the right response? Did they act in ways that were different from their usual behavior? Then, ask them to discuss their memory recall process –

■ □ ■ □ ■

what part of their memory was easy or hard to recall? Were they too embarrassed to remember everything or too embarrassed to tell everything they remembered?

Now, ask participants to think of a time when they worked the hardest in very engaging and intense work—perhaps after little sleep and in spite of being drained. Again, with a partner, have them discuss what the reason or reasons were for the effort. Ask questions to discover if their efforts were because they valued the work or because an outside agent valued the work. Was it for a degree (school work), was it for art (a showing was coming up), or was it for peer response (I'll show them who can do it)? Ask participants to compare and contrast why some work went easier and some harder. Look at not only the content but also the emotional state of the learner.

Ask participants to discuss the two emotional states— anger and engagement—in relation to memory and learning. Talk about how the emotions help create cognitive patterning for long-term retention. Enlist reflections and insights from the group.

Focused/Peripheral: Learning Principle 3

Learning Principle 3:	Learning involves both focused attention and peripheral perception.

A Story to Tell

A daughter was running late for her father's birthday party. She had to stop by the department store to pick up an engraved gift. Her sisters had told her and told her to get this done ahead of time, but she had put it off until the day of the party. Now, she had twenty minutes to stop at the mall, run to the gift department on the third floor, get the gift, and get over to her father's house. She would have to really move it.

Frantic, she directed her husband into the mall parking lot. He doubled parked, and she ran as fast as she could in her high heels. She sped through the cosmetic department on the first floor, up the escalator, past men's wear to the second floor, and through the women's fashions on the third floor to the gift department. At the

Synonyms—Focused Attention

Converging

Concentrating

Zeroing in on

Homing in on

Noticing

Regarding

Synonyms— Peripheral Perception

Background

Secondary importance

Milieu

Surrounding

Perimeter

Outer part

counter, she showed her ID, grabbed the bag, and ran back down the way she had come.

She jumped into the front seat of the car, set the gift in the backseat, and said to her husband, "Let's go."

"So, you got it okay, right?" the husband asked. He had seen his wife struggle many times to master the concept of time management.

"Yeah, I got it and we will not be late, but you know something?" she asked.

"What's that?"

"I told my sister that the fall fashions for women were going to be heavy on orange and show lots of suede, and that is just what they are showing."

"What are you talking about?"

"The fall fashion line is out, and I noticed lots of orange and lots of suede as I was rushing through the store. It's hard not to notice, even though my mind was focused on getting the gift."

Things You Need to Know

What's It All About?

As the story shows, the woman focused on a single, important task but also was able to absorb other information that was in her peripheral sphere. The brain takes in all kinds of sensory input, not just what it is attending to. Peripheral vision allows people to see beyond the targeted focal point and to pick up shadows and objects on the side. The brain sweeps the knowledge environment like the eye sweeps the landscape. It picks up all kinds of sounds, images, smells, and tactile sensations. The brain's radar is tuned both to direct, explicit information and to implicit, less obvious information.

The brain's radar is tuned both to direct, explicit information and to implicit, less obvious information.

The brain processes thousands of bits of information, mostly registered by sight, every second. It constantly decides the importance of incoming information based on the focus of the person. As the brain absorbs incoming information, it connects the conscious and unconscious levels of processing. Processing occurs through both focused attention and peripheral perception.

Something being learned through focused attention is affected by peripheral perception like a grape is affected by the soil in which it is grown. The soil's contribution comes out in the final tasting as hints, shading, and subtle flavors. The same is true for peripheral perceptions: memory acquires pointers, blends, and subtle connections from the information gathered peripherally. In other words, information is contextual, and that context is the periphery of the targeted focus.

For example, when we are talking with someone and we enter a crowded room, in order to continue our conversation, we raise our voice, move closer to the person to adjust to the clusters of the other people, take smaller steps, and turn our shoulders to move —but the whole time, we are listening closely to our partner. Later, we may remember the music in the crowded room, the number of familiar faces, whether people were wearing coats, and if they were eating or drinking—all information garnered from the periphery of our attention. It is through peripheral perception that we process all of the information that, if attended to, would overload our focused attention. Peripherally, we are able to take in important sensory stimuli that is a vital part of the learning process. We know more and we learn more than what we focus on.

Why Bother?

It is important that teachers are aware of and are deliberate about the peripheral environment in the learning situation.

Students are as aware of the context surrounding the lesson as they are of the lesson itself. Based on this idea, it is important that teachers are aware of and are deliberate about the peripheral environment in the learning situation. In this way, they can take advantage of this dual processing through intentional "trappings" that support the lesson.

Through the work of Marian Diamond (1999), we know that an enriched environment helps grow dendrites (the components of the brain cell networks that comprise memory and learning) and that it stimulates brain activity. Based on this principle of the brain, teachers strive to create environments that are not only enriched, but also are environments that contain relevant instructional materials, presented in novel and interesting ways. Students can interact explicitly and implicitly with this environment.

Because students make connections in their mind in their own way and in their own time, Diamond believes from her research that the learning environment should be ever changing. The brain is stimulated by novelty. A changing environment fits the concept of a good learning environment. If the periphery is important to learning, then it makes sense to keep changing it as the focused attention of the learner changes. The materials in the environment must evolve from the curriculum if they are to enhance learning. Brain-friendly learning environments include music, colors, manipulative materials, linguistic and non-linguistic representations, and a variety of seating options. Soft couches, throw pillows, or raised private areas to sneak away to often add to students' learning environment by presenting novelty and opportunity for movement and change.

On another level of peripheral perception, that is, the emotional level, students sense safe environments, respond to teachers who speak in respectful tones, and adjust their own behavior to fit into the environment in which they find themselves. When a classroom environment supports learning with sensory-rich surroundings, students may be better able to make meaning of new material at their own pace and in their own way. Figure 3.1 shows a number of classroom items that enhance novelty and stimulate students' learning.

Figure 3.1. Classroom periphery.

Bulletin boards	Tone of voice	Facial expression	Room arrangement
Black- or whiteboards	Music	Body language	Furniture
Classroom view	Background noise	Proximity	Temperature
			Lighting

A Tiny Transfer to Try

Environmental Issues

Introduce the idea of focused attention and peripheral perception, with special attention to the enriched environment. Pair participants. Explain that first, they are going to write and talk about the importance of an enriched environment that surrounds their formal lesson and instructional focus. Ask them to divide a single sheet of notebook paper into three sections: (1) My Preferred Learning Environment, (2) My Preferred Teaching Environment, and (3) Best Idea for Creating A Learning Environment.

Start with the first section, which addresses teachers' awareness of the environment for their own learning and how they prefer to study. Ask them to think back to their school days – and describe, briefly, how they studied. Was it in a library, dorm room, listening to music, watching TV, or other habits?

Next, ask the teachers to consider the teaching environment. Have them jot down ideas about the environment in which they prefer to teach. Ask them to think of their first classroom. How have their classroom bulletin boards changed since they began teaching? How are they different today? What shifts have they made?

Finally, share the *best idea* that they ever had for creating a good learning environment. Have them describe what changes they made. How did it work out? How did they know it was a good idea? What proof do they have in terms of student behavior/achievement?

■□■□■

After both partners have had a chance to jot down their thoughts on the three learning environments, have them share their ideas.

Close with a summary comment from each about the power of peripheral learning as part and parcel of focused learning.

PART TWO: SKILLS OF LEARNING

Again, revisiting the Caines' twelve principles, the authors have selected three principles specifically for the second quadrant, Skills of Learning. The three principles that seem to fit into the idea of skillful teaching (instruction) include: Principle 4, The brain learns part to whole simultaneously; Principle 5, The brain has spatial and rote memory systems; and Principle 6, The brain is a parallel processor.

All three of these principles speak to the concept of direct instruction in which the teacher uses effective instructional practices. For example, remembering Principle 4, the skillful teacher intentionally teaches some skills in isolation before blending them into an application. For example, students learn about adverbs and then they write adverbial phrases in their essays. Along the same line, teachers tap into rote memory patterns with explicit practice, repetition, and rehearsal and, at the same time, they take advantage of spatial memory pathways by embedding the learning in an experience. For instance, students learn their multiplication facts and use them in a puzzling problem. And, finally, harnessing principle 6, teachers use the fact that the brain is a parallel processor by using multimodal instructional strategies. To illustrate, students working in the chemistry lab are bombarded by sights, sounds, and smells as well as taste and touch as all the four lobes of the brain are at work.

This quadrant on Skills of Learning comprises the three principles that seem key to powerful and effective instructional input from the teacher. Skills of Learning is about content standards that include mathematics, science, and all the disciplines; about life skills, such as thinking, socializing, and problem solving; and about all the things teachers are accountable for in terms of the curriculum. It is all about skillful teaching.

Parts/Whole: Learning Principle 4

Learning Principle 4:	The brain simultaneously perceives and creates parts and wholes.

A Story to Tell

A fourth-grade teacher has spent the spring teaching her class all about bugs and insects. During a week of good weather she decides to take the class on a field trip to the Botanical Garden, a local attraction. All of the students have their notebooks with sketches of the insects that they might find among the shrubs and flowers. Some of them have magnifying glasses and butterfly nets while others carry binoculars and field glasses.

The day of the trip is a wet and sunny spring day, perfect for walking through the hills and valleys of the beautiful botanical gardens. The maple trees that line the parking lot have small light green leaves that hang heavy with morning dew. Although the sun has dried the cement walkways, the teacher asks her students to stay on the path.

Synonyms — Part

Component

Fraction

Detail

Segment

Piece

Factor

Synonyms — Whole

Totality

Completeness

Entirety

Unity

Synthesis

Big picture

They walk through the front gate and, stretched out before them, see the magnificent main gardens with beautifully designed flowerbeds that shine in the mid-morning light. The gardens are split by red brick walkways, bordered with dark green hedges.

The students spread out and start looking closely at the foliage and searching for insects, hoping to find one they have studied in the classroom.

A girl looks out on the view and says to her teachers, "Miss Henderson, who made all of this?"

"It was planned by the city more than fifty years ago. It's based on a design in Hyde Park in London."

As they spoke, two boys approached them. One of the boys cupped in his hand a pile of moist black soil. In the middle of the soil was a long wiggling earthworm.

"Look, look at this. Look at the size of it."

The girl screeched and stepped back. The teacher held her hand and said, "No, look at what they have. Out there," and the teacher pointed toward the gardens, "Out there are thousands of worms, and little bugs and insects. All of them are part of this. You can't see it now but they are all part of this beautiful place. They are the myriad parts of the whole ecosystem that result in the beauty of the plants, flowers, and trees that we see."

■ □ ■ □ ■

Things You Need to Know

What's It All About?

Teaching often involves explaining ideas by taking them apart and reducing them to their smallest components, for example, letter sounds for words, notes for melodies, and parts of speech for sentences. For optimal learning, the brain needs a context, a synthesis, or big picture, to connect the discrete information into a bigger chunk. It must connect the parts of a skill-and-drill lesson to the embedded application within the whole.

For optimal learning, the brain needs a context, a synthesis, or big picture, to connect the discrete information into a bigger chunk.

Each person lives in the world as he or she finds it. Making sense of information delivered at 1500 bits a second would be impossible if humans did not have a way to simultaneously process the big idea, the landscape, the whole of the subject and, at the same time, process the parts, the components, the bits. The world can be messy and, if brains did not have the capacity to sift through, to make sense of, and to connect all of the sensory input that they are faced with, life would be, if not impossible, at least much harder. Perhaps this concept is captured best in the saying—We can't see the forest for the trees.

When driving, the driver sees the details on the map, but also sees the bigger picture and how the directions will make sense as he actually sets out on his way. A reader, when reading a single word, sees its spelling and, at the same time, sees how it fits in the context of the sentence, the paragraph, and the story. It is about right and left

■□■□■

hemisphere processing. The right processes holistically, whereas the left processes analytically, by taking things apart.

Humans are always putting the "parts" together with the "whole." This processing is automatic and involves mental as well as physical learning systems. A golfer can practice her swing for hours and, as she does, is preparing to apply the refined swing to accomplish the larger goal of playing a good round of golf. A musical theater actor builds his act in parts: he learns lyrics, then the music, then the stage blocking, and finally the dance steps—all with the aim of pulling it all together in a performance. During the preparation, the actor learns the components that are part of the final performance as well as preparing for the final performance.

> **Humans are always putting the "parts" together with the "whole."**

Why Bother?

To teach to the brain so that it sees both parts and wholes, teachers must orchestrate learning through complex tasks that require both analysis and synthesis. It is not enough to teach about adverbs in a discrete and separate way, even though that analytical approach provides manageable bits. To be more brain-friendly, learning must draw students to use individual adverbs in a whole way—in their writing—so that they can understand more completely how to apply their understanding of adverbs. Adverbial phrases are the result of learning about the separate and discrete adverbs.

In the classroom, teachers always have to connect the skill and skill activities to the larger context. Having students working only on the parts of speech, names of state capitals, or table of elements without teaching where these things fit into the whole is not brain friendly. The brain can and wants to process parts and whole simultaneously. It wants to fit the pieces into the whole context because learning is contextual.

In the classroom, teachers always have to connect the skill and skill activities to the larger context.

Students who ask, "How will I use this?" could simply be trying to understand the new information in a larger context. When students are challenged by projects that require them to learn facts as part of a larger goal, they find relevance and are motivated to learn. Mastering the rules of weights and counterweights is easier when applying the information in a real world situation. When reading a novel or story, details learned as part of the tale become anchored when the brain remembers them together, as part of the same learning experience. Figure 4.1 shows a number of part to whole matches in different learning contexts.

Grammar: Composition In composing, go back over an essay and pick out the parts of speech. Move back and forth from writing and dissecting the parts to studying the parts and then writing.

Calculating: Story Problems In calculating, read the story problem out loud, discuss, and try to solve it verbally. Take the same story problem and break it down on paper, separating each of the different calculations; then, work on each one separately. Finally, reconstruct the story to solve the problem.

Keyboarding: Word In keyboarding, type specific words that exercise specific finger combinations, then type whole paragraphs with similar combinations that occur naturally in the essay.

Dates: History In history, have a student play the role of George Washington, using wig, costume, and set design. To be interviewed by a news reporter, the student has to master the facts of George Washington's life.

Skeleton: Human Body   Students learn the name of different muscles and bones and then watch a video of athletes using those same muscles and bones. Or, students learn the name of muscles and bones and, at the same time, they touch and examine a skeleton to feel the real thing.

Figure 4.1. Parts and whole in different learning contexts.

A Tiny Transfer to Try

In Sequence

Divide participants into groups of three or four. Have each group choose a physical skill to be taught, preferably one that involves a few different intelligences (a dance step, a tennis serve, etc.).

Ask the group to break the skill into five to eight essential parts. Next, ask them to describe each part on a separate sheet of paper – but not to number the parts or indicate the order of the parts in any way.

After 15 minutes, have each group scramble the order of their instruction sheets and leave their stack on the table. Then, ask another group to choose an instruction stack other than their own, reconstruct the proper order for the instructions, and prepare to demonstrate the skill.

After all groups have demonstrated a skill, ask them to think about how they put the instructions in order. Have them discuss how important it was to know the skill's name to understanding the parts of the skill and how useful their personal knowledge of the skill was in sequencing the skill. Urge them to discuss how the principle of part and whole applies to this activity.

■ □ ■ □ ■

Spatial/Rote: Learning Principle 5

Learning Principle 5:	There are two types of memory systems: spatial and rote.

A Story to Tell

In the movie *Jaws*, the salty sea captain, Quint, has to decide whether to bring the town sheriff and the college-educated oceanographer, Hooper, with him on his boat as he sets out to get the killer shark. He is upset by the idea of taking an unproven sailor with him and challenges Hooper to prove he really is a seaworthy sailor. Quint doesn't ask Hooper for references or to relate past experiences but instead throws him a length of rope and says, "Tie me a sheep's head."

Hooper says to the sheriff, "Been a while since I had to pass basic seamanship."

Synonyms—Spatial

Natural

Experiential

Three-dimensional

Location

Related

Contextual

Synonyms—Rote

Separated

Practiced

Memorized

Committed to memory

Impressed

Learned by heart

■ □ ■ □ ■

Things You Need to Know

What's It All About?

The brain is equipped with an automatic memory system, called spatial memory. This spatial memory imprints what the person experiences. These memories are embedded in the brain and need no rehearsal to be recalled. On the other hand, rote memory is not automatic. To recall discrete facts and data, the brain needs practice, rehearsal, and repetition. The brain learns best when it encounters novelty, finds an emotional connection, or when the event is embedded in a natural, spatial experience. When learning things that do not fit into those categories, it is best to learn them by rote.

Rote Memory

The rote spatial memory system is necessary to memorize information not embedded in natural spatial memory. One way to think about how the rote memory system works is to imagine a front yard with green grass. The mailman walks across the lawn once a day, six times a week, but leaves no trail. The grass shows no sign that anyone walked on it. But, the three children and the father who live in the house daily cross from the garage to the front door without walking on the stone footpath, following the same exact trail. Soon the grass is worn, showing a clear track where they have been walking. Over time, they have killed the grass and created a permanent path. This path development is similar to how the neural pathways are formed for rote memory and learning.

■ □ ■ □ ■

Rote learning can be motivated by an upcoming public display of knowledge, a test in school, a speech, or it can be emotionally driven by personal motivation. For example, when you want to remember a license plate number or the name of an artist on a CD, you use your rote memory system.

To memorize information by rote, it is best to work in small chunks, to drill for intense periods of time while always respecting the positive affects of rest on the brain. Drilling for four separate 15-minute periods is more useful than drilling for one 60-minute period.

To memorize information by rote, it is best to work in small chunks.

Rote learning works best when applied to a procedure or a skill. When a procedure or skill is rehearsed again and again, it becomes a habit. We rehearse the skill until it becomes embedded in our long-term memory. Then, we can perform the skill almost without thinking. It becomes automated through our neural network.

Connecting new information to prior knowledge or fitting new information into patterns familiar to the brain are both good strategies for learning, but, when learning by rote, unrelated facts can be learned at the same time. It is possible to learn the address of a residence and the distance between two planets at the same time, if the learning is done by rote exercise.

Spatial Memory

Spatial memory is characterized by the image of Hansel and Gretel walking deeper and deeper into the dark forest. At each cautious step they take, they soak in each sound and sight. Their foolproof plan to mark their return path has been spoiled by the bread-eating birds, and now they are overcome with emotions. Their senses become heightened, and readers believe as they read the story that Hansel and Gretel will never forget this walk in the woods—and neither will the reader.

Spatial memory works best when there are new things to learn. It builds on what has already been learned, connecting new information to old, creating a whole, complete, unforgettable experience. Because the mind has almost endless capacity for learning, it can absorb, process, and integrate new spatial memory constantly. The brain naturally takes in the details of its environment, orienting itself to new spaces, but this process may shut down in the case of extreme fatigue, when a person is just too tired to know where they are.

The mind has almost endless capacity for learning.

Novelty is a vital part of the spatial memory system. For example, an ever-changing landscape of mountains, waterfalls, and snow-capped peaks spied from the back seat of a moving car is much more interesting than one cornfield after another. Emotion plays a big part in the spatial memory system. When we return to a specific place, in our mind or in fact, we not only remember facts about the place but we remember smells, sounds and emotions. Try taking a walk, real or in memory, through your grade school and note the many sensual memories that arise.

Why Bother?

To encourage the brain to remember experiences automatically in its spatial memory system, teachers need to create as many authentic or virtual experiences as possible to facilitate student learning. But, when the brain needs rehearsal to remember what is learned by rote memory, drill-and-skill exercises are a necessary evil.

Rote learning has its place in a high-achieving classroom. Even during novel and authentic learning, procedures learned repetitively have their place. If a class takes a science field trip, the setting may be novel and interesting but they will have to be able to set up and use a microscope. This skill is best taught through rote until the procedures become a habit.

Teachers need to be careful how they use rote learning as it can slide quickly into mindless drill-and-skill activity. Sometimes when students learn simple facts (dates, names, figures) by the rote method, it is best to teach them with a sing-song rhythm or with a rhyme. This helps slot the information into a familiar pattern. For example, try to say the alphabet without singing. The beat and melody of the tune is easier for the brain to remember.

The spatial memory system works by engaging the mind and then anchoring new information through novel, interesting interaction with the material. Learning involves the entire physiology and so students who are moving, using their hands, talking, and listening are more likely to activate the entire memory system. This spatial learning in inexhaustible and is the way man learns naturally. In fact, part of man's evolution can be traced to the point where he learned that repetition, beyond instinct, made his life better.

In a classroom, when teachers see authentic wonder on the faces of their students, they know that these learners are immersed in the learning and that they will remember what they learned.

Spatial learning in classrooms is exemplified by the following examples:

Social Studies or Language Arts: Put on part of a costume—perhaps just a hat—change posture, and use an accent to get into character or create an historical figure of the era.

Science laboratories: A student walks into the area where the animals are kept, and the smells and sounds trigger a memory that reminds him to weigh, water, and feed them.

Manipulatives: Plastic science toys that are designed to model molecules make the learning easier as the students add or remove chemical chains that change the properties of the molecule.

Excursions or field trips: There is anticipation that creates an emotional hook. There is visual and spatial novelty that gets the brain's attention. There is a change of procedure so students cannot be on automatic pilot. There is an expectation that students will have to bring back some knowledge or an artifact from the field trip.

Virtual field trips: If the mind believes that it is experiencing something, then its memory system reacts as though it has really experienced it.

Rote learning is captured in these typical examples:

Mathematics facts: Mastering mathematics involves understanding and applying rules at the proper time. A way to remember the various rules is with sayings or rhythm, for example, "Yours is not to reason why, just invert and multiply."

Spelling: Spelling sometimes does not seem logical to new learners and so educators give them memory cues, for example "i before e except after c."

A Tiny Transfer to Try

Down Memory Lane

Have participants work in pairs. Ask them to identify themselves as A or B. Then, ask the As to turn to their partners and hypothesize on why a student will sit in the same seat every class, or why a member of an exercise class will position him- or herself in the same place every time. Then, ask them to apply their hypotheses to their classrooms. Do they stand in the same place in their classroom? Do they use the same room arrangement day in and day out? Do they arrange the teaching materials in the same way from year to year? What happens when they must use a different classroom? After this discussion, debrief the concept of spatial memory and the power of being in that same space for learning situations.

Next, ask the Bs to teach their partners something they learned by rote. Ask them to explain how they learned the piece by rote memory. Ask the Bs to reflect on how the experience of rote learning feels and what kinds of learning it best suits.

Take a moment to compare and contrast the two types of memory pathways: spatial and rote.

Parallel Processing: Learning Principle 6

Learning Principle 6:	The brain is a parallel processor.

A Story to Tell

An eighth-grade student sits at her computer in her bedroom looking for a reference to include in her essay on the American Revolution. Her focus is on scrolling through the Internet, page by page, marking in the bookmark section sites that might be helpful, while in the upper right hand corner of her screen, she follows her friends' conversation in a chat room. Occasionally, she clicks into the chat room and types in a pithy comment and then returns to the Web search.

She wears a set of headphones loosely around her neck to hear a recording of George Washington's first inaugural speech. She wants to memorize the speech and, when she recites the speech in class, will video tape it for her portfolio.

Outside her window she can see her younger brother shooting hoops with his friend. If the friend's older brother shows up, then she will figure out a reason to walk outside and visit.

Synonyms — Parallel

Lined up

Aligned

Collateral

Analogous

Correlative

Comparable

Across her desk is a stack of pages she has ripped from fashion magazines, sorted according to ones she likes, ones she thinks she likes, and ones she knows she doesn't like. She has to decide on what she is going to wear to a party in three weeks and right now she has no idea.

Behind the student, the television is showing videos with the sound muted, but if a good video comes on, her chat room friends tell her (they all are watching the same channel) and she will use the remote to turn up the volume.

This parallel integration is the reason humans can understand complex new information while creating new ideas quickly and almost without effort.

On her knee is an ice pack because she has to ice her knees after soccer practice, 10 minutes each knee, three times. To help her prop her leg up, she has her foot on a soccer ball and she rolls it around in small circles.

Through her open bedroom door she hears her mom's voice, "What are you doing up there?"

"Nothing," she answers.

Things You Need to Know

What's It All About?

The brain processes information through the four lobes simultaneously, almost unconsciously, integrating the sights, sounds, thoughts, and other sensory input that it encounters. This parallel integration is the reason humans can understand complex new information while creating new ideas quickly and almost without effort.

■ □ ■ □ ■

The brain's four lobes—the frontal (cognitive function), occipital (visual function), the parietal (sensory/motor function), and the temporal (auditory function)—work in concert, seamlessly. For example, you are watching a band and suddenly the musicians stop playing and the singers continue. You instantly become aware of how much the music added to the singing, although while you were listening you had taken this for granted. It is when certain expected stimulation is absent that people are most aware of the how these lobes interact.

The brain is a parallel processor, which means it is able to multitask—that is, do several, even many, functions at once. This integration happens naturally. For example, sounds are recognized as words, the words are organized into sentences, the sentences form a thought, a response to the thought is prepared, how the response might sound is considered, and finally, the response is made out loud.

As the brain receives sensory impulses, it handles the information both viscerally at the feeling or emotional level and cognitively at the rational level. The brain processes this information analytically or critically and, at the same time, creatively, looking for ways to connect ideas.

Why Bother?

One implication of the ability to process different stimuli in parallel is an inherent need for more complex tasks that engage multiple senses and that foster conversation between the two hemispheres of the brain, processing in linear and in holistic ways. When the brain encounters robust, rich, and rigorous tasks, it is challenged to analyze (to take ideas apart)

> **When the brain encounters robust, rich, and rigorous tasks, it is challenged to analyze and to synthesize.**

and to synthesize (to put them together). Think about it. Parallel processing is what occurs when the learner is problem solving, making decisions, or creating and inventing.

Teachers who design instruction that challenges students are doing them a favor because the brain responds, naturally, to complex problems. When classroom instruction involves simply one or two types of information processing (listening passively, writing notes during lectures), the brain is coasting. When the same students are involved in meaningful conversation, creating a graphic organizer of information, writing and reading with a purpose—using their brains to full capacity—they are more engaged in the learning.

The classroom environment can naturally support the parallel processing among the teacher's direct instruction, the students' cooperative strategies, and the information on the walls of the classroom. As part of the same activity, students listen to the teacher as expert, hearing vital instructions. The students also are engaged in the task at hand in their groups, planning, predicting, listening to each other, reading notes, referring to their texts, doing what needs to be done to accomplish the goal. At the same time, they are immersed in a classroom that is novel and interesting. The brain processes and integrates the three sources of information to make sense of what it is trying to learn.

Some argue that this multi-sensory environment might be, for some students, too complex with too many things happening at the same time. But, if studies have told us anything, it is that students are more likely to be bored or uninterested in the learning and that, more often than not, they simply are not engaged, intellectually or emotionally. Goodlad (1980) documented this phenomenon in his seminal study of 1,000 high schools. He basically concluded that students were docile thinkers and passive learners who definitely were bored in their classrooms. To encourage the processing of information in the four lobes of the brain simultaneously, teachers must consider the idea that there needs to be a challenging curriculum that involves rigorous and meaningful instruction.

A Tiny Transfer to Try

Olders and Elders

Use the essay, "Olders and Elders," shown in Figure 6.1. Explain that the assignment involves doing three different treatments of the story: First, simply count the different people mentioned in each category—olders and elders. Second, list the characters mentioned on a time line. And, third, create a non-linguistic representation of the story.

Instruct the participants to work in teams of three to four participants to complete the tasks. Suggest that as they work, they track their parallel processing of the parts of the story and the entirety of the story. Ask them to discuss: How do both hemispheres come into play and whether all four lobes are involved in the problem solving?

People reading anecdotes of early Glendale must wonder at times whether Glendale was that unusual, considering the events related and the people described, or if it was just another small town.

They may be right. Maybe you could find similar situations and people elsewhere but where else would you find another community that had, living directly across from each other in a small valley, two families named Older and Elder.

No one seemed to think this unusual. In fact, I don't recall anyone ever remarking on it until the year of the Pioneer Days celebration when a little squabble developed between the two, and that wasn't over the similarity in their names.

Each outlying area of Glendale was to provide two representative residents from one family — one from the original stock and one from the second generation. The only rule was that the family with the greatest age gap between the two representatives would be selected, sort of like the point spread in football.

The Elder family thought they had the nomination won hands down until the Olders claimed that the older Elder was not older than the elder Older. The Elders countered by pointing out that although that may be true it was only by a few years whereas the younger Older was so much older than the younger Elder that the difference wiped out the advantage of the elder Older over the older Elder.

In fact, the Elders said, they could put up the younger of the two older Elders and still show a greater age differential. But the Olders stood pat on the elder Older advantage and sought to discredit the fact of the younger Elder being ahead in points over the younger Older and they would not enter into any comparison using the younger older Elder bit.

Finally a compromise was reached whereby the elder Older and the older Elder, with the younger Elder added, would represent the valley.

It was a good thing that the Pioneer Days celebration was held that year because the following year, the old Clark place, which was nearby, was occupied by a family named Younger.

Leslie Pete
Portland, Oregon

Figure 6.1. The olders and the elders.

PART THREE: INTERACTIONS WITH LEARNING

For the third quadrant, Interactions With Learning, three of the Caines' principles that apply are Principle 7, The brain involves the entire physiology; Principle 8, Each brain is unique; and Principle 9, Learning is social and embedded in experience. All three seem aligned with the idea of active and interactive learning that accompanies authentic experiences.

Principle 7's premise that the brain involves the entire physiology speaks to the idea that teaching includes facilitating learning through awareness of the mind/body connection. Hungry, tired, stressed learners are not as open to the learning situation. Skillful teachers are aware of this physical aspect of learning.

Similarly, knowing that the brain is uniquely organized by a person's experiences is also critical for effective teaching. Principle 8 emphasizes that it is because each brain is wired differently and each brain continues to change its structure and its chemistry through a process called plasticity (Diamond & Hobson, 1998) that teaching presents a daunting challenge for educators. To tap into the various entry points in these unique brains, teachers often apply Gardner's (1983) framework of multiple intelligences as a necessary component of classroom practice.

And, finally, this quadrant embraces the concept of facilitating learning by recognizing the need for social influence (Vygotsky, 1978) and the power of experiential learning (Dewey, 1938). In essence, quadrant 2, according to the authors, says, "We teach," whereas quadrant 3 says, "They learn."

Physiology: Learning Principle 7

Learning Principle 7:	Learning engages the entire physiology.

A Story to Tell

An earnest middle-age investment banker retired early so he could become an elementary school teacher. He entered an accelerated Master's program and soon was part of a team of new teachers practicing in a summer session with second and third graders.

This banker-cum-teacher was very serious and believed in the benefits of a good education. He was going to work in an urban school near his home and thought that his students were going to be very much like the kids he had seen every day on his way to the bank. He believed he knew what they needed and that he could give it to them.

> **Synonyms—Physiology**
>
> Living system
>
> Organism
>
> Human body
>
> Bodily systems
>
> Biological systems
>
> Living organism

In the summer program, he was working with a group of second- and third-grade students, seated six at a table. He sat at one end and leaned over and pointed into the books in front of the students. Speaking in a very serious tone, he explained the concept of verbs and nouns and gave examples that made sense to him. As he continued to talk, he noticed that the children seemed to shrink back in their seats. His voice became strained, and he began to sound frustrated. He tried hard to sound patient, but it was becoming clear that the kids did not understand what he was trying to teach them.

In the hot classroom, students slumped down and seemed tired, but the teacher continued explaining key points of the lesson that he thought he needed to tell them so that they could learn.

As he was talking to a boy to his left, a third-grade girl got out of her seat and walked behind the investment banker/teacher. She placed her hand on the middle of his back and began to rub it up and down slowly. Sensing his stress, in a low voice she said, "It's OK, don't worry, it will be OK."

Things You Need to Know

What's It All About?

The research on the brain is informing many things that educators do in their classrooms. One thing it has affirmed is the idea that the brain and the body are one living organism. What happens to one affects the other.

The brain and the body are one living organism.

Learning engages the entire physiology, both brain and body. It involves cognitive, affective, and physical domains. An emotional response is characterized by a change in heart rate, blood pressure, and breathing, as well as thinking. There is no separation between the mind and the body. Specific areas of concern about the mind/body connection include emotions, nutrition, relaxation, and exercise.

Emotions

The emotions guard the gate of learning. Reassuring words said in a calm voice help students learn not because of what was said but how it was said. Students feel better emotionally, thus their brain functions more optimally. A safe environment is one in which students can take a chance and feel that they will not be embarrassed. This crucial link between emotions and intellect is key in the discussion of the brain as a living system.

Nutrition

In addition to emotional well being, there is the effect that good nutrition has on the brain's ability to function. A diet that is well balanced, without empty calories such as those provided by refined sugar, helps students think. Protein in the morning, light nutritious snacks throughout the day, and plenty of water is a great way to enhance student achievement. Although this type of diet may not be possible in all situations, attention to the role of nutrition in the learning process can help teachers diagnose problems in the classroom.

The keys to good nutrition can be part of the curriculum. The science of how good food helps students think might make a fine poster or handout to take home and hang on the refrigerator door. When students understand for themselves the cause and effect of good nutrition, then teachers have laid the groundwork for lifelong learning, health and fitness.

Relaxation

The brain also needs down time to relax and form lasting deep connections to new information. A day that is designed with some quiet time for reflection allows the mind and body to rest and to process. Even though students spend much of their time sitting, they can become exhausted mentally after a strenuous day of schoolwork. Their body and mind need an opportunity to stretch and relax. Students who seem to space out during a video or lecture may just be processing or making connections from knowledge from a previous learning experience. To honor the brain as a part of the whole body means to give the brain time to think deeply and to rest.

Exercise

Physical exercise plays a vital role in promoting optimal learning. When the body is exercised vigorously, it oxygenates the brain for optimal functioning. Adults understand the role exercise plays in a complete lifestyle. Students' needs are no different.

Figure 7.1 gives some tips on how to encourage achievement by thinking of the body and brain as one system.

■ □ ■ □ ■

Nutrition

Favor high protein breakfasts

Avoid sugar, sweets, and carbohydrates

Drink lots of water

Choose crunchy snacks (celery, carrots)

Relaxation

Find quiet times (2-3 minutes)

Use music to foster easing up

Consider visualization techniques

Explore emotional intelligence

Exercise

Stand and stretch frequently

Exercise vigorously for 20 minutes

Exercise regularly, daily if possible

Exercise with the family, for fun

Figure 7.1. Tips to enhance student performance.

Why Bother?

The idea that students' physiological make-up and needs affect learning is not new by any means. Because brain research on learning reinforces the importance of nutrition, exercise, and relaxation, the opportunity is ripe for re-examination of current practice.

Brain research on learning reinforces the importance of nutrition.

Schools throughout the United States are reconsidering their relationship with food service companies that stock the vending machines with soda pop and insist on fast food as the primary item on the cafeteria line. The policy of selling candy to raise funds for extra-curricular activities is also being questioned.

Implications for more explicit education about nutrition, provisions for frequent physical activity throughout the school day, and the benefits of periods of relaxation seem pertinent for improving optimal learning.

Students who understand that their ability to think is influenced by a good night's sleep, balanced meals, relaxation, and regular exercise may be intrinsically motivated to alter their own behavior.

Thinking takes energy and can cause fatigue. Movement is one way to combat this fatigue. But, there is more to encouraging physical movement in the classroom than just recess or playtime. Allowing students to move about on their own, to sit on the floor, to sit on their knees on the chair, or to stand and lean on the desk are all simple ways that encourage the learners to learn in ways that they feel are most comfortable. This is not a recipe for poor classroom management. On the contrary, students finding ways that help them engage in learning leads to a well-managed classroom.

Students finding ways that help them engage in learning leads to a well-managed classroom.

■ □ ■ □ ■

A Tiny Transfer to Try

When to Move

In a workshop setting, before–not right before but before–lunch, have the teachers do a sitting and thinking activity. Make the topic deep and pretty difficult. For example, ask them to plan a mediated journal entry about their *favorite learning style*. Give them time to write, ask them to share with another, and then have them share within the group.

After lunch, do the same activity but now have the mediated journal entry be about a *difficult learning experience* – a time when learning did not go very well. Ask them to sit down as they do this activity. As they are about half way through, energize the experience by changing the exercise. Ask them to get up and participate in a "People Search" on the same subject, "Times when learning was tough." Ask them to find four different people to talk about these four situations:

1. Has had a writing block and can explain how they overcame it.

2. Can name three brain-friendly foods and explain why they work.

3. Can explain how to get endorphins flowing.

4. Can describe how sugar works in the body.

Now, have the whole group discuss the physiological effects of trying to think while (a) sitting down *before* lunch, (b) sitting down and working *after* lunch, and (c) moving around in the classroom and discussing ideas with colleagues.

Brain Uniqueness: Learning Principle 8

Learning Principle 8:	Each brain is unique.

A Story to Tell

Two fifth graders, Joe and Pat, are walking home from school. Joe's younger brother, Ted, is walking with them with his head down.

Joe is talking to both of them about what he learned in biology.

"And they say that the human body continues to grow at least until you are 18 years old, and that our DNA is the most complex combination of chemical combinations that has ever been discovered."

**Synonyms—
Uniqueness**

Sole

Original

Novel

Individual

Only

Unduplicated

"You said combinations twice," Pat said.

"What?"

"You said complex combination of combinations."

"I didn't," Joe said.

Without looking up Ted said, "You did, combination of combinations, I heard it."

"Anyway, it doesn't matter–the point is each of our DNAs is as different as our fingerprints. There is not one of us that is exactly like any other one of us."

"You said the brain keeps growing until how long?" Ted said as he walked with his shoulders slumped, head down.

"They said, your brain starts growing before you are born and . . ."

"I don't know about you," Ted interrupted, "But for me, my brain started growing before I was born and didn't stop until I got to long division."

Things You Need to Know

What's It All About?

People start their lives with their own DNA and, as they grow, their brains wire themselves based on the connections they make through their own experiences. Because people do not travel the same path in life, each has his or her own combination of wiring. Humans are different from each other and all have their own particular ways of reacting to the world. This distinction in the way individuals think and feel is why the brain organizes itself differently for each of us and why each brain is as unique as a thumbprint.

Each brain is as unique as a thumbprint.

How individuals respond emotionally is also determined by their past experiences and how these experiences, good or bad, have shaped the way they think. Because emotions are such a powerful determinant of how new information is processed, the wiring of the brain may have as much to do with the heart as with the mind. Consideration of how a learner feels about a subject is as important as what he or she knows about it.

According to Gardner (1999), the human brain is organized differently for each person. Each has a "jagged profile" of multiple intelligences, and the strongest ones provide entry points for learning. Gardner has identified eight intelligences, although he cautions that there may be more. Among the ones recognized are verbal, visual, musical, mathematical, bodily, interpersonal, intrapersonal, and the naturalist. One of these intelligences may be more dominant than the others, but all intelligences are present to some degree in each of us.

A group of students can attend an event, such as a field trip, and come away with very different, even contrary, perceptions about the day. These perceptions or memories differ because each person has a unique set of neural connections and even though the experience is virtually the same for all of the students, each processes the events in his or her own way. Consequently, their memories of the event differ from those of the other people.

Why Bother?

The principle of brain uniqueness speaks directly to the concept of differentiated instruction. The effective teacher exhibits a robust repertoire of strategies that is ongoing and ever growing. These skillful teachers know how to tap into the talents of different students. They know how to use a variety of entry points in the teaching/learning process. Grounded in the knowledge that each brain is unique, these teachers are well prepared to implement different teaching models in their classrooms as a matter of course.

Differentiation is essential in today's classroom not only for diverse, special populations but for all students. Experience tells educators that different children respond differently in each situation. Some are auditory learners, some do better with the written word, and others are hands-on learners.

Differentiation is essential in today's classroom.

The traditional classroom often favors those students who are strong in the verbal/linguistic and mathematical/logical intelligences. Not surprisingly, teachers who are comfortable in a traditional educational setting are often also strong in these areas. However, to reach all of the unique brains in the classroom, skillful teachers make an effort to think differently about all the ways people can learn and to accommodate the various entry points in these learners.

An optimal classroom allows each student to explore and discover the curriculum in a way that is natural for that individual. Students who are making connections in their own way are more apt to accept new approaches to learning. Skillful mediation engages students through different learning styles and teaches them things that are way beyond the subject matter. Differentiated instruction is about more than reaching each student—it's about reaching each where he or she is and helping each move to a new place.

Students who are making connections in their own way are more apt to accept new approaches to learning.

A Tiny Transfer to Try

Smart Graph

Have teachers form a human graph on three points that summarize Gardner's intelligences:

One: "School Smarts" (Verbal, Naturalist, Math)

Two: "Art Smarts" (Spatial, Bodily, Music)

Three: "Personal Smarts" (Intrapersonal, Interpersonal)

Ask members of each point to discuss among themselves why they picked that spot. Then sample their rationale as a group.

After discussing the responses to the Smarts Graph, ask the groups to consider how they were taught in school. Was their style of learning honored in the school they attended as young children? Create another human graph to respond to the statement: My learning style was honored in school. Ask participants to move to one of five positions on the scale: strongly disagree, disagree, not sure, agree, strongly agree. Then, ask them to discuss and share why they selected the particular level of agreement or disagreement.

Finally, ask how their classroom, as teachers, is open to the different types of learners in the world. For example, a teaching repertoire includes strategies for curriculum design, instruction, and assessment. Curriculum design comprises integrated curriculum, problem-based learning, and thematic units. Instruction encompasses direct instruction, cooperative learning, multiple intelligences, and graphic organizers. Assessment involves traditional, portfolio, and performance methods. How do they, as teachers, alter the teaching and learning and assessment in their classroom to accommodate the principle that every brain is unique? How do they differentiate in these areas?

Social/Experience: Learning Principle 9

Learning Principle 9:	The brain is social and understands and remembers best when facts and skills are embedded in natural spatial memory.

A Story to Tell

Rick and John sat around the kitchen table eating breakfast. Their mother, standing by the sink, asked them how school was going.

"OK," said Rick. "I got an A on the math and might get an A on the essay."

"Essay, essay on what?" his mother asked.

"It's about a guy who stays in the woods and writes about life. It's in, no, it's near a pond."

"Walden Pond?"

"Yeah, that's it." Rick answered and kept eating.

"What does he say about the life?"

"Who?"

Synonyms — Social
Gregarious
Civil
Bonded
Shared
Allied
Interactive

Synonyms — Embedded
Included
Ingrained
Set
Captured
Meshed
Enveloped

"The guy in the woods, what was his name?"

"I just wrote the essay, Mom, I didn't memorize it"

"Oh, I see. John, how is school for you?"

"OK."

"Any classes you like?"

"Science stinks."

"Oh, well, you know, it's just one class, and sometimes there are subjects we might not like at first. What's wrong with science?"

"Nothing, it stinks, that's why I like it. We do stuff in science, like last week, a group of us did an experiment. We learned how to make copper react with hot concentrated sulfuric acid in a flask. The copper dissolved, forming sulfur dioxide gas. As the flask cooled, atmospheric pressure forced water from a second flask into the first one, dissolving the sulfur dioxide. It was all about chemical reactions giving off energy in the form of heat and pressure. It's part of theme we're doing on the balance in nature. It's pretty cool, and it smelled neat."

"Oh, I see," his mother says, "Chemistry stinks, but that's good!"

Things You Need to Know

What's It All About?

Because humans are social animals, it just makes sense that their brains will develop in social situations, spurred on by the reactions and emotions of those around them. Watch an infant around his or her parents. You see some things about the infant that are inherited, like hair color or facial features, but you also see that most of the child's behaviors or mannerisms are derived from mimicry. Children learn from their parents how to act in the world. This learning from others continues throughout human lives. Paraphrasing Vygotsky (1978), we learn first in a social setting and then we internalize the meaning in our own minds.

Whether a child or an adult, people take their cues unconsciously or consciously from other people in most situations. They quickly observe and process facial expressions, body language, mood, tone, and content of the conversation to determine what is the norm. They react to this stimulation first by feeling and then by thinking. They determine how they are going to stand, what their face will show, what they will say, and how they will say it.

> **People take their cues unconsciously or consciously from other people in most situations.**

Significant socialized learning is embedded in experience. Teachers know that humans learn best when they learn by doing. A concept or abstract idea can never be fully mastered until it has been learned in a concrete way, which is frequently learning by doing. Learning is context-bound. The situation in which learning occurs helps imprint that learning on the learner's spatial memory system.

The principle of sociality basically means that memory is facilitated when discrete information is embedded in dialogue and authentic learning experiences. Memory is enhanced through the real or virtual experiences of the learner because experience places the memory in the spatial memory system, which is the brain's automatic memory. It is associative memory, that is, associating with a place, episode, or experience.

Humans are constantly processing information about the world around them. This spatial orientation is the most powerful and dependable learning humans do. Learning embedded in social experience gives a learner's brain situated learning. The brain is applying past information to new situations, helping learners decide what they want to do, how to do it, what to say, and how to say it.

Memory is evidence of learning, and learners' most powerful memories are ones in which they were fully and physically engaged in the experience. Watching a lion tamer in a circus is informative, but if the watcher were invited into the cage to participate, the event would be much more memorable because he or she would experience the situation fully. Listening to someone tell how to do something or reading about how to do something is not as memorable as doing it. When learning at the computer, the learner wants to do the moves. The learner wants the mouse! It makes the learning more engaged and more memorable,

> **Learners' most powerful memories are ones in which they were fully and physically engaged in the experience.**

Why Bother?

Knowing that the brain remembers best when facts and skills are embedded in natural spatial memory, teachers need to orchestrate learning through authentic student tasks. In addition to authentic tasks, opportunities for students to engage with other students helps them process and to fully realize learning potential.

There are many projects that students can do alone to have the experience of embedding the learning in natural spatial memory. There is a place for this in any robust and rich curriculum. A trip to the forest to observe nature, take field notes, and be alone to journal is an example of a solitary project that is about learning by doing. In addition, to pursue complex challenging projects, working in cooperative groups is so effective because it adds the element of the social brain.

> To pursue complex challenging projects, working in cooperative groups is so effective.

Effective cooperative groups are powerful for learning in the classroom. Assignments can be rigorous and robust, engaging students by requiring them to use facts and skills to accomplish a goal. Working collaboratively requires group members not only to function as a team but also to understand the importance of learning in a social setting. It is fairly evident that reading or passively watching does not engage the mind fully but that actively participating in a stimulating problem-solving session does.

Emotional security in cooperative groups can be achieved by teaching social skills (Johnson, Johnson, & Holubec, 1986). As they become comfortable and feel safe, students think more effectively. Positive emotions shared among classmates increase the intrinsic motivation to learn. The learning becomes anchored in experience and good emotional memories.

These tasks are often referred to as performance tasks and are accompanied by predetermined criteria for quality. Examples of performance tasks include creating a newspaper about a country or region, constructing a model bridge to hold a predetermined weight, or creating a musical for an historic time. At the beginning of the assignment, the goal of the group may be to simply get a passing grade, but, as they become more involved in the project, their ideas spark enthusiasm that drives more learning than they might have thought possible. The memory of the experience—the combination of facts learned and emotions felt—becomes embedded in the long-term memory system.

A Tiny Transfer to Try

Up Close and Personal: Architects of the Intellect

Use the article that appeared in *Educational Leadership* (Fogarty, 1999) titled "Architects of the Intellect", or visit the web site *www.robinfogarty.com* to find Architects of the Intellect.

Divide the group into eight smaller groups. Select 8 architects from the 13 (Coles, Costa, Dewey, Diamond, Feuerstein, Gardner, Goleman, Montessori, Perkins, Piaget, Pinker, Sternberg, and Vygotsky) available on the web site or use the 8 architects in the article. Explain that each group is going to use the information in the article or from the web site to create a panel of architects. One member from the group represents the group's architect, while the other members assume supporting roles. The roles of the group are:

1. The actor who plays the architect in a panel discussion.

2. The manager who coaches the actor and can offer answers.

3. The researcher(s) who collect facts about the architect and his or her opinions

4. The illustrator who creates a poster of the panelists book.

Encourage the actors to dress in costume, use props, and affect the mannerisms of the architects. Engage other participants as much as possible in the event. Additional roles for group members might include Prop Master, Question-Maker, and Encourager.

Each team is required to submit a list of five questions to the Moderator (teacher) to be asked during the panel discussion. When the panel is ready, allow each architect an opening statement that presents his or her basic theory. These opening comments are brief, but are to be as specific as possible to differentiate each theorist from the other. The moderator also encourages panel members to dialogue with each other and debate points as panelist respond to questions from the audience. For example, Gardner and Goleman might discuss how their theories are similar or different.

PART FOUR: LEARNING ABOUT LEARNING

In the final quadrant, Learning About Learning, three principles from the Caines' twelve seem to cluster logically in this learning-to-learn, metacognitive arena. These include Principle 10, The search for meaning is innate; Principle 11, The search for meaning occurs through patterning; and Principle 12, Learning involves both conscious and unconscious processing. All three are anchored in the concept of deeper processing and reflective thinking.

Principle 10 speaks to the intuitive nature of the human brain in its quest to make sense of the world. The brain naturally seeks meaning—this is, in essence, its nature.

Similarly, Principle 11 suggests the power of that search for meaning is the nature of the human brain. It scans the inner horizons for patterns that fit with the incoming ideas. The brain deliberately and intentionally looks for similarities that match post experience and prior knowledge. And the final principle, number 12, addresses the inherent processing features of the human brain that occur even in the unconscious. The brain seeks explicitly to continue to process implicitly in its resting state. In fact, it is believed that deep processing occurs when one is in deep sleep (Sejnowski, 2003). Quadrant 4 is the reflective arena of the teaching/learning process. And, it is in this reflective mode that learning is personalized. This is where real transfer of learning occurs as the learner puts the ideas to use in meaningful ways and anchors the learning for long-term memory and storage.

Meaning: Learning Principle 10

Learning Principle 10:	The search for meaning is innate.

A Story to Tell

Jake was in the library after school, beginning work on an assignment on the role of Whigs in early American government. In an effort to stay awake, he brought in a cup of tea from the cafeteria. As he laid out his books, he noticed the label of the tea bag hanging from his cup, Earl Grey. He opened a dictionary, went to Whigs, and read it was an18th- and 19th-century British political party that was opposed to the Tories. He wasn't sure what a Tory was so he looked up Tory and discovered that during the period of the American Revolution, a Tory favored the British side and was also called a Loyalist.

> **Synonyms — Innate**
>
> Inborn
>
> Instinctive
>
> Intrinsic
>
> Natural
>
> Automatic
>
> Fundamental

This—being a loyalist—seemed like a positive thing, but he always understood that in the American Revolution, being loyal to Great Britain was bad. So he looked up *loyalist* and read that one of the definitions was, "One who supported the established government of Spain during the Spanish Civil War."

■ □ ■ □ ■

Jake loved Hemingway and knew he had fought in the Spanish Civil War. Following his interest, he looked up *Spanish Civil War*, where the town of Guernica caught his attention. When he looked up Guernica, he discovered that Picasso had created a famous painting called Guernica, and that in his last testament, Picasso stipulated that the painting might be returned to Spain only after the return of democracy.

Jake looked up the word *democracy*, which took him back to the Whigs but also mentioned the Tories again, the opposition party to the Whigs. He searched for the Tories again and discovered that there were many British Prime Ministers from the Tory Party, including Earl Grey, who won the general election in 1830.

Jake closed the book, took a sip of tea, and started thinking that maybe he had something interesting to write.

Things you Need to Know

What's It All About?

The brain seeks to make sense of the world. It is a powerful, natural life force that drives humans to constantly evolve and adapt to their environment. The search for meaning is developmental and learning follows learning in a never-ending pursuit.

This fundamental drive is obvious in small children who pick up and examine everything within their reach. This curiosity is spontaneous and always is ignited by what gets their attention. Objects that children pick up that do not hold their attention are dropped in favor of the next thing.

This need to make sense of the world, to pursue the questions they can't answer, and to solve the riddles that baffle them is a characteristic that follows humans throughout their whole life. This search for meaning is part of the natural functioning of the brain.

This search for meaning is part of the natural functioning of the brain.

There is nothing more confounding than to be stumped in a mystery story, to have a plot turn on a clue you might have missed. A stumped reader will read and reread a story to discover how he might have missed a clue. This need to find out where he was wrong is an example of the innate search for meaning. People have to discover for themselves why and how the logic of a story escaped them. The personal satisfaction they feel when they make meaning of the puzzle is a sweet and lasting sensation.

Among the many ways the brain tries to make meaning of new information is by trying to match incoming data with existing patterns already formed. If there is no matching pattern, the brain keeps searching to identify, categorize, and sort the data in a meaningful way. This patterning is critical to memory and learning.

Patterning is critical to memory and learning.

Another aspect of the search for meaning is emotional relevance. Humans are intrigued by what they determine is emotionally valuable. If they believe that new information serves their emotional needs, makes them feel good or safe, they are invested in deciphering and storing it for future use. Relevance serves the search for meaning!

■ □ ■ □ ■

Why Bother?

What this principle asks teachers to keep in mind is that, in the classroom, they can guide this life force with confidence. In spite of the sometimes lackadaisical attitude of children, humans naturally are inclined to learn. In fact, their brains need to learn to grow. This is what their brain is designed to do.

To lead the students to new heights of achievement, teachers find it imperative to make the learning fresh,

Teachers find it imperative to make the learning fresh, relevant, and challenging.

relevant, and challenging. When children are bored, they lose interest. If they lose interest, they will not pay attention. Nothing is as boring to a child as old news. The expression "Been there, done that" is a perfect encapsulation of this idea. Teachers must constantly tease students with new ways to approach old ideas, if they are to hold the interest of their students.

A fertile classroom environment includes word games, visual puzzles, books and resources from grades far above the grade level—deep open-ended philosophical ideas that raise the bar, that invite and entice the brain to learn. An atmosphere that invites learning is structured in a way that allows students to wander mentally, to feel free to follow their muse. Sponge activities (engaging activities) that involve transition times in the classroom or between classes may result in students being so involved that they will find it almost impossible to return to the schedule of the class. These magical moments are to be cherished as the child is feeling a connection that may change his attitude about learning forever. Csikszentmihalyi (1990) calls this level of total immersion, *flow*, a state when time passes unnoticed and quickly because of a sense of enjoyment and fulfillment.

Sample performance tasks that engage the natural curiosity and search for understanding are shown in Figure 10.1.

- Demonstrate "a million" in a concrete mode.
- Develop a travel brochure for a region of the country.
- Devise a guided tour for a museum.
- Create a Rube Goldberg invention.
- Design a web site.
- Dramatize a story.
- Stage a musical.
- Publish a newspaper about "A Decade."

Figure 10.1. Sample performance tasks.

Some criteria for assessing performance tasks include:

1. Accuracy of content

2. Degree of completion.

3. Quality of product

4. Impact of presentation

5. Timeliness of completion

6. Demonstration of process

7. Relevance of subject

A Tiny Transfer to Try

Oxymora! Optical Illusions!

To experience the principle that the search for meaning is innate, consider expressions in popular language in which two very different words are linked to form a very sensible expression: jumbo shrimp, icy hot, or tears of joy. These oxymora cause the brain to think, to reason, and to make meaning of something that literally seems contrary and confusing.

Working in A-B pairs, have the partners create at least three oxymora. Ask volunteers to share some of their creations with the whole group.

Then, show the optical illusion in Figure 10.2 of the "old woman/young woman." Let the pairs discuss the "mental gymnastics" of seeing one image and then shifting to the other image.

Figure 10.2. Optical illusion.

Patterning: Learning Principle 11

Learning Principle 11:	The search for meaning occurs through patterning.

A Story to Tell

Joe walked into a keynote address at a teaching conference, and the speaker had already begun. He opened his notebook, checked the subject of the session, and then began to listen, ready to take notes. The speaker was saying,

. . . variable resistors are used to set the neural weightings in this implementation. If one is set midway, then the associated input would have no effect on the system because the voltage would be evenly applied between the two op-amp inputs, resulting in a weighting of zero. Set the potentiometers toward the top, and the op-amp is positively biased. Since op-amps have a natural threshold of zero volts difference, an extra bias input is required. Any number of additional inputs and potentiometers may be inserted . . .

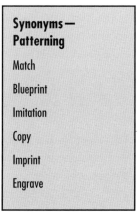

Synonyms—Patterning

Match

Blueprint

Imitation

Copy

Imprint

Engrave

Joe stared down at his empty notebook and back up at the speaker. He said to himself, "This is not making sense. I signed up for this conference, and now I am sitting here trying to understand but I cannot make heads or tails of what he is saying." Joe continued to listen, hoping for something to hook into . . .

> To create a large neural network, one could either construct thousands of op-amp circuits (like the one in the photograph) in parallel, or one could merely simulate them using a program executing on a conventional serial processor. From a theoretical stance, the solutions are equivalent since a neuron's medium does not affect its operation.
>
> And that is something I learned the hard way only recently. You see, I have two sons who both went off to college and their experiences show how much of what I have been saying is true today.

Aha! Joe thought he sensed a pattern—a narrative with an expected outcome that will illuminate the speaker's point— and he thought the speaker had hinted at the structure—a comparison of his two sons. This is something Joe understood because it is a familiar pattern, and he expected to comprehend what he had heard so far by making connections with the story the speaker was about to tell. Joe became more comfortable and anticipated a certain level of comprehension. The lecture began to have relevance, and he felt more confident that he would be able to hook into the point the speaker was making.

■ □ ■ □ ■

Things You Need To Know

What's It All About?

When information comes into the brain, it activates neural pathways that might be a possible fit for the material. If an appropriate pattern is not found immediately, the brain continues to try to slot the idea somewhere, somehow. If there is no place to slot the information, there is a good chance it will never get in. If a learner says something that does not make sense, he or she might as well be saying it does not fit into a pattern.

Patterns are a set of characteristics that seem to go together to form relationships on some level. Determining the relationship requires comparing and contrasting the information and then aligning it into a schema. Things learned through patterns are reinforced through familiar themes, structures, or connections. If someone hears a seven-digit number, such as 2334512, she remembers it by using the same pattern she uses with a phone number, that is, three digits followed by four digits: 233 – 4512.

When teachers present new information to learners, learners have more success when they can relate it to something they already know. To a large extent, that is what the human brain does naturally. Prior knowledge refers to facts and patterns, making what is known as important as how it is known. Storage of information in long-term memory provides the framework for how learners store and catalog information in the real world. Warehouses, databases, and libraries work on a system of consistent

> **Learners have more success when they can relate information to something they already know.**

dependable rules and procedures. Users have confidence in their search for information in these systems because the systems mirror how human brains store and classify facts and concepts.

Using patterns to search for meaning is demonstrated by how humans think. For example, if Mike asks Susie for directions to drive across town, Susie might respond by asking, "Do you know where this landmark is?" She is prepared to give directions or some new information, presented in a familiar way, but first she tries to determine what Mike knows in order to know where to begin the pattern.

Why Bother?

It just makes sense to provide the patterns whenever possible.

If the brain is searching for meaning through patterning, it just makes sense to provide the patterns whenever possible. These patterns often come in the form of themes, rules, principles, theorems, concepts, skills, and procedures. These patterning devices help students generalize the learning for future applications.

Helping students make connections is helping students learn. This simple idea is dynamic in action. The brain slots new information based on existing patterns, causing a change. Connections form new connections and the brain, at a chemical and electrical level, comes alive, firing neurons to help solidify dendrites and anchor new information in long-term memory.

Think about the use of patterns in school and in life and consider how teachers might use them to help students learn. This overarching attitude can help teachers in a school teach with themes that really help form connections. In a higher order thinking classroom, teaching with patterns in mind also encourages students to infer or anticipate as they follow the logic of a pattern. It helps them understand the rules of design that are dependable in a good system. Learning to recognize patterns and make meaning with them builds confidence as students see order where there might have been chaos.

> **Teaching with patterns in mind also encourages students to infer or anticipate as they follow the logic of a pattern.**

Thematic instruction is a great way to introduce big ideas that can be repeated throughout a school year. This thematic approach naturally feeds into the brain's desire to make meaning through patterns. These themes may vary, but each student will make sense of them in their own way. Broad ideas, while different, have consistent characteristics that support a pattern, order, reason, or cause and effect. Examples of themes include change, structures, decades, culture, bridges, relationships, tradition, rituals, exploration, and habits of mind.

In addition to class-wide themes, students find reinforcement in their own efforts and as patterns are repeated, from one subject to the next, from one class to the next, and from one year to the next. Satisfaction leads to a better emotional state and optimal performance. The brain operates as it is designed to by slotting new information into familiar patterns and creating connections that result in deeper understanding and cognition.

Patterns also can be presented in ways that appeal to the many types of learning styles that are present in a classroom. Students can experience examples of information in patterns in different media, such as the visual, the musical, or the tactile. The overriding implication is to use patterning as often as possible in the classroom and to help students see the explicit

Use patterning as often as possible.

patterns in what they are studying. If, in addition to explicit patterns, teachers also teach students that their brain wants to organize information in patterns, then students will become more aware of how their brain stores information for learning.

A Tiny Transfer to Try

Form pairs. For each list, ask partners to choose which word does not fit.

1. Monkey	Swim	Pony	Rhinoceros
2. Swede	Afghan	Maltese	Boxer
3. Hazel	Brown	Temple	Auburn

Now, ask partners to come up with their own examples. Ask for volunteers to share their examples. Then, discuss Principle 11, The search for meaning occurs through patterning.

1. Swim is not an animal; Rhinoceros is not a dance.
2. Swede is not a breed of dog; Boxer is not a nationality.
3. Hazel is not a college or university; Temple is not a color.

Conscious/Unconscious: Learning Principle 12

Learning Principle 12:	Learning always involves conscious and unconscious processing.

A Story to Tell

The teacher, Mr. Tucker, sat on his desk and said to his class of middle school students, "Let me tell you a story."

"In 1971, I was fresh out of college, I had everything in my car and was trying to decide if I should go to Phoenix, where I had a girlfriend. Well, I thought she was still my girlfriend."

The class laughed and Mr. Tucker smiled, took a drink of coffee, and continued with his standard lecture on the value of looking for the inspiration.

"So, I am driving through Texas on the way to Arizona. I stopped at a gas station to fill up and get a candy bar or something."

"Mr. Tucker needed a caffeine fix," said one of the boys in the back row, and everyone laughed.

> **Synonyms — Conscious**
>
> Intentional
>
> Knowing
>
> Attentive
>
> Purposeful
>
> Deliberate
>
> Focused
>
> **Synonyms — Unconscious**
>
> Subconscious
>
> Unpremeditated
>
> Unaware
>
> Instinctive
>
> Unintentional
>
> Involuntary

"No, in those days it was only gas stations with, maybe, a vending machine." Mr. Tucker continued, "But at this gas station was this travel book on New Mexico. As I picked it up, I spotted a story about Santa Fe, this cool looking city. I read how it was a nice place to live."

"Maybe," I thought, "I might get a teaching job there. Maybe this would be a better choice for me."

"So, I'm back on the road riding along through West Texas and I come to this railroad crossing. I am stopped at the crossing by the lowering of the crossing bar. I'm stuck there, waiting and watching this long freight train rumble past the windshield of my car."

"And I am working the question over in my mind. Should I go to Phoenix and try to keep something going or go to Santa Fe and start something new? I wasn't sure, and so I sat there watching this freight train blow by my windshield at 60 miles an hour. And because this was a train from the Santa Fe Railroad, on the side of every car in big bright white letters were the words, "Santa Fe.'"

"I'm sitting there thinking, 'Should I drive to Phoenix?' and right in front of me is the words, Santa Fe, Santa Fe, Santa Fe, over and over, just flashing right before my eyes. Well, as you can figure, I never made it to Phoenix."

Things You Need to Know

What's It All About?

The brain never stops processing the sensory input that bombards it. Although we may not be consciously aware of it, our brains attempt to solve the problems that we present it. This constant processing sometimes results in answers that seemingly come out of the blue but, in fact, were percolating in our frontal lobes until all of the information came together.

Constant processing sometimes results in answers that seemingly come out of the blue.

Conscious Processing

Conscious processing is facilitated by making connections more explicit through deliberate attention to reflections that tie into the problem at hand. Of course, conscious processing occurs as the learner is working with new material and the mind is trying to make sense of it. It is important to develop habits that encourage quiet time so that the brain has the opportunity to work with available information to process new input. If the quiet time occurs consistently, at regular intervals, the brain can literally adapt and prepare.

Develop habits that encourage quiet time.

Unconscious Processing

Another role that quiet time plays in conscious/ unconscious processing is the familiar one of allowing information to perk to the top. Sometimes, when we work hardest on a problem, the answer seems to elude us, but when we start doing something completely unrelated, the answer comes to us. The ability to walk away from a vexing problem, with confidence, is the sign of someone who understands the inner workings of the brain and that it needs time to make connections.

■ □ ■ □ ■

Yet, there is other unconscious processing that goes on as well. Even when one is asleep, there is deep processing of information (Sejnowski, 2003). Unconscious processing occurs 24 hours a day, 7 days a week, 365 days a year. The brain, like a shark, never sleeps. That's why that "brilliant idea" awakes you at 3 a.m. The brain is constantly working to make sense of the input and to try to find the pattern, the connections, and the insight.

Even when one is asleep, there is deep processing of information (Sejnowski, 2003).

If the brain continues to process new information by reinforcing existing neural connections even while we sleep, then it makes sense that this processing occurs on a much more varied time schedule. People may take days or weeks to understand a lesson they were supposed to learn in one afternoon. Some people, in certain areas of their life, might "get it" right off the bat but not be able to understand other things for weeks.

Why Bother?

The most obvious implication for the classroom is for teachers to foster the conscious and unconscious processing of information. Support may be structured times for individual reflections in journals and logs, reflections through dialogues, or whole group debriefings about an important idea. Teachers can foster conscious processing with the use of a mediated journal in which the teacher provides cueing labels for journal entries. In this way, they guide students to be more open to possible solutions that they were not aware of before.

Teachers can help students explicitly look for connections to what they already know and explore how to use the new information in meaningful ways. This can easily become a lifelong learning skill as the students become confident in their ability to look inward for answers they trust will be there. Being aware of the unlimited potential of our own brain is a very powerful feeling. It can breed confidence, which is a strong emotion to have during a learning experience. Explicit attention to processing involves affective, cognitive, and meta-cognitive strategies. Figure 12.1 lists several techniques to use to help students make connections explicitly.

Teachers can help students explicitly look for connections to what they already know.

Affective Processing
Plus, Minus, Interesting (PMI)
Aha! Oh, No!
Journals

Cognitive Processing
3-2-1 Contact (Recalls, Insights, Questions)
KWL (Know, Want to know, Learned)
Learning Logs

Metacognitive Processing
What? So What? Now What?
Mr. Parnes' Questions
    How does this connect?
    How might I use it?

Mrs. Potter's Questions

  What was the goal?

  What went well?

  What would you do differently?

  Do you need any help?

Mr. Pete's Pointers

  What else?

  Tell me more.

  Give a specific example.

Mrs. Poindexter's Prompts

  What was easy?

  What was hard?

  Where did you get stuck?

  How did you get unstuck?

Figure 12.1. Techniques for fostering connection-making.

A Tiny Transfer to Try

Harnessing the Invisible

Working in A-B pairs, have each partner prepare a quick story on how they tapped into their ability to solve a problem by walking away from it.

Then, gather ideas from the entire group about how to "harness the invisible" (unconscious processing) in problem solving.

BIBLIOGRAPHY

Ausubel, D. (1978). *Educational psychology: A cognitive view* (2nd ed.). New York: Holt, Rinehart, & Winston.

Bloom, B. S., Engelhart, M. S., Furst, E. J., Hill, W. H., & Kratwohl, D. R. (1956). *Taxonomy of educational objectives: Cognitive domain, Handbook 1.* New York: David McKay Co.

Bruer, J. (1999). *Myth of the first three years: A new understanding of early brain development and lifelong learning.* New York: The Free Press.

Burke, K., Fogarty, R., & Belgrade, S. (2002). *The portfolio connection* (2nd ed.). Thousand Oaks, CA: Corwin.

Caine, G., Caine, R. N., & Crowell, S. (1999). *Mindshifts: A brain-compatible process for professional development and the renewal of education* (2nd ed.). Tucson, AZ: Zephyr Press.

Caine, R. N., & Caine, G. (1991). *Making connections: Teaching and the human brain.* Alexandria, VA: Association for Supervision and Curriculum Development.

Caine, R. N., & Caine, G. (1994). *Making connections: Teaching and the human brain.* New York: Innovative Learning Publications, Addison-Wesley Publishing.

Cooney, W. C., Cross, B., & Trunk, B. (1993). *From Plato to Piaget: The greatest theorists from across the centuries and around the world.* New York: University Press of America.

Csikszentmihalyi, M. (1990). *Flow: The psychology of optimal experience.* New York: HarperPerennial.

D'Arcangelo, M. (2000). The scientist in the crib: A conversation with Andrew Meltzoff. *Educational Leadership, 58*(3), 8–13.

Deming, W. E. (1986). *Out of the crisis.* Cambridge, MA: The MIT Press.

Dewey, J. (1938). *Experience and education.* New York: Collier Macmillan.

Diamond, M., & Hobson, J. (1998). *Magic trees of the mind: How to nurture your child's intelligence, creativity, and healthy emotions from birth to adolescence.* New York: Dutton.

Eisner, E. (1979). *The educational imagination: On the design and evaluation of school programs.* New York: Macmillan Publishing.

Feuerstein, R. (1980). *Instrumental enrichment.* Baltimore: University Park Press.

Fogarty, R. (1999). Architects of the intellect. *Educational Leadership, 57*(3), 76–78.

Fogarty, R. (2001). *Differentiated learning: Different strokes for different folks.* Chicago: Fogarty & Associates.

Fogarty, R. (2001). *Student learning standards: A blessing in disguise.* Chicago: Fogarty & Associates.

Fogarty, R. (2001). *Teachers make a the difference: A framework for quality.* Chicago: Fogarty & Associates.

Fogarty, R. (2002). *Brain compatible classrooms* (2nd ed.). Thousand Oaks, CA: Corwin.

Fogarty, R. (2002). *Making sense of the research on the brain and learning.* Chicago: Fogarty & Associates.

Fogarty, R. (2003). *A look at transfer: Seven strategies that work.* Thousand Oaks, CA: Corwin.

Gardner, H. (1983). *Frames of mind: The theory of multiple intelligences.* New York: Basic Books.

Gardner, H. (1999). *Intelligence reframed: Multiple intelligences for the 21st century.* New York: Basic Books.

Goleman, D. (1995). *Emotional intelligence: Why it can matter more than IQ.* New York: Bantam Books.

Goodlad, J. (1980). *A place called school: Prospects for the future.* New York: McGraw-Hill.

Gopnik, A., Meltzoff, A., & Kuhl, P. (1999). *The scientist in the crib: Minds, brains, and how children learn.* New York: William Morrow.

Hannaford, C. (1995). *Smart moves: Why learning is not all in your head.* Arlington, VA: Great Ocean Publishers.

Hart, L. (1983). *Human brain, human learning.* Kent, WA: Books for Educators.

Haycock, K. (1999). *Good teaching matters...a lot.* Oxford, OH: National Staff Development Council.

Hyerle, D. (1996). *Visual tools for constructing knowledge.* Alexandria, VA: Association for Supervision and Curriculum Development.

Jensen, E. (2000). *Brain-based learning: The new science of teaching and training* (Revised ed.). Thousand Oaks, CA: Corwin.

Jensen, E. (1999). *Teaching with the brain in mind.* Alexandria, VA: Association for Supervision and Curriculum Development.

Jensen, E. (2000). Moving with the brain in mind. *Educational Leadership 58*(3), 34–37.

Johnson, D. W., Johnson, R. T., & Holubec, E. J. (1986). *Circles of learning: Cooperation in the classroom.* Alexandria, VA: Association for Supervision and Curriculum Development.

Joyce, B. R., & Showers, B. (1983). *Power in staff development through research and training.* Alexandria, VA: Association for Supervision and Curriculum Development.

Joyce, B. R., & Showers, B. (1995). *Student achievement through staff development* (2nd ed.). White Plains, NY: Longman.

Kagan, S. (1989). Cooperation works! *Educational Leadership, 47*(4), 12–15.

Kerman, S. (1979). Teacher expectations and student achievement. *Phi Delta Kappan 60*(10): 716–718.

Kohn, A. (1993). *Punished by rewards.* New York: Houghton Mifflin.

Kotulak, R. (1996). *Inside the brain: Revolutionary discoveries of how the mind works.* Kansas City, KS: Andrews and McMeel.

LeDoux, J. (1996). *The emotional brain: The mysterious underpinnings of emotional life.* New York: Simon and Schuster.

Lyman, F., & McTighe, J. (1988). Cueing thinking in the classroom: The promise of theory-embedded tools. *Educational Leadership, 45*(7), 18–24.

Marzano, R., Norford, J., Paynter, D., Pickering, D., & Gaddy, B. (2001). *A handbook for classroom instruction that works.* Alexandria, VA: Association for Supervision and Curriculum Development.

Marzano, R., Pickering, D., & Pollock J. (2001). *Classroom instruction that works: Research-based strategies for increasing student achievement.* Alexandria , VA: Association for Supervision and Curriculum Development.

Mensa Quiz. (January 15, 2003). *American Way,* pp. 72–73.

Miles, M., & Huberman, A. B. (1984). *Qualitative data analysis: A sourcebook of new methods.* Beverly Hills, CA: Sage.

Motivation and rewards [electronic booklet]. (2001). San Diego, CA: The Brain Store. Available from www.thebrainstore.com

Parnes, S. (1975). *Aha! Insights into creativity.* Buffalo, NY: DOK Publications.

Pete, B. M. & Fogarty, R. J. (2003). *Nine best practices that make the difference.* Thousand Oaks, CA: Corwin.

Piaget, J. (1954). *The construction of reality in the child.* New York: Basic Books.

Pinker, S. (1997). *How the mind works.* New York: W.W. Norton.

Robinson, F. P. (1970). *Effective study.* New York: Harper & Row.

Rowe, M. B. (1974). Wait time and rewards as instructional variables, their influence on language, logic and fate control: Part 1. Wait-time. *Journal of Research in Science Teaching, 11,* 81–94.

Senjowski, T. (2003). *Learning while sleeping* [speech]. San Diego, CA: Brain Expo.

Sousa, D. (2001). *How the brain learns* (2nd ed.). Thousand Oaks, CA: Corwin.

Sprenger, M. (1999). *Learning and memory: The brain in action.* Alexandria, VA: Association for Supervision and Curriculum Development.

Sylwester, R. (1995). *Celebration of neurons: An educator's guide to the human brain.* Alexandria, VA: Association for Supervision and Curriculum Development.

Sylwester, R. (1999). *Student brains, school issues: A collection of articles.* Thousand Oaks, CA: Corwin.

Sylwester, R. (2000). Unconscious emotions, conscious feelings. *Educational Leadership, 58*(3), 20–24.

Varlas, L. (2002). Getting acquainted with the essential nine. *ASCD Curriculum Update* (Winter), 4–5.

Vygotsky, L. (1978). *Mind in society.* Cambridge, MA: Harvard University Press.

Walberg, H. J. (1999). Productive teaching. In H. C. Waxman & H. J. Walberg (Eds.), *New directions for teaching practice and research* (pp. 75–104). Berkeley, CA: McCutchen Publishing.

Westwater, A., & Wolfe, P. (2000). The brain compatible curriculum. *Educational Leadership, 58*(3), 49–52.

Wolfe, P. (2000). *Brain matters.* Alexandria, VA: Association for Supervision and Curriculum Development.